Dedication

This is dedicated to the changing of an ungodly, anticipated event so that it will not happen due to this new course of action that can stop the process of negativity in its tracks and to bypass it in order to be at a place to receive the blessings of the Lord, as it is meant.

Please understand that Bound to Heaven Publishing/Ministries is not trying to put any kind of fear in anyone pertaining to the subject matter we are informing the public about. If by chance, someone does feel a little reserved about this process of thinking that has been explained, this may be a good reason for you to acknowledge the process of what can happen if there isn't something done about it to help stop a possible calamity of some kind from happening.

M-N
Don't get caught up in the willy-nilly, it isn't really worth it.

M-N
Don't get tired of studying

M-N
Dare to land on a new Island with a book

M-N
Stop the Travel

If you don't know where you are going, any road will take you there.

People can learn to stop big business and politics that creates the oil sands in life which are destroying a part of life that people can never repair or replace. It will also help stop the untimely deaths of people. Do the math and learn to take a loss at the right times in life.

Foreword

This is a part of your invitation to participate in what can and will protect our election process. Your ticket and complete script is within the book titled, *The Devil Passed Me By*.

Use this presence of thought to comfort you in your quest of belief to add others as the Lord sees fit for you to do. From a single action one should not draw from it a state of existence that the consequence for the universe is failure that is foolish in life because with the use of wisdom we are free.

To stop the ungodly fight that Satan has plans for. The facts are all politicians and their families involved in this common process or not need to be briefed on this matter especially if you have faith in the Lord.

The logistics have their place but the reality of it can be grim if we don't take heed to the warning signs that are being given.

Although there is more mention of the Republican National Convention, the presentation of this information has been developed for the Democratic Party as well. There is no mystery that a newly developing kind of race for the office of president includes both parties. That person will represent the people of the USA for at least four years, if not eight.

Now we can't deny the fact that the Democratic party may find themselves in a similar race that could call for a contested vote for the nominee to determine who will represent the people. If it becomes a contested issue, we can be prepared to act on. it is a change that Satan wants to become a part of to tear down and hurt people at the same time. Therefore, the same perception applies, no party pooper (Satan) is allowed. We must use the same tools to stop the intruder in the name of Jesus.

To Clear the Air

To put the defogger on in order to not be running into each other, there must be something put in place; a new kind of light. The light has to be made to not just do one thing, but it must cut through the atmosphere of negativity that could become a part of the convention.

This process of disagreement will take some of the people involved to an uncomfortable level of disgust, anger, emotional struggle and to a level of losing control. When you add this up it is already the stuff the witches stew and warlock brew is made out of. That is why we don't need to add more to this recipe for what could be a blend of a volcano eruption that could spill over and damage everyone around.

We are imploring the people at the party to come aboard to a state of mind that can help to protect all involved. This will include the whole body of people in the convention, all people of the media. This will also include the people who came in with the politicians, everyone on the inside and outside.

The breeding ground for Satan's fury is not to be placed under pressure. That is what we are doing; releasing the pressure before the dam bursts.

We need to be on one accord to stop the ungodly fold from the opportunity to get a toehold on the party and start dragging people down to cause a hell raising that will harm anyone it can, it being the prince of darkness b/k/a Satan. This is why you are requested to be the peace of the union with the other three that is needed to stop the spiritual warfare from happening in the process.

This book is for the people as well as the politicians. It can help lead the way to make it all good in the neighborhood.

The use of names of any and all people, places and/or things contained within this book are strictly unauthorized.

Welcome to a State of Using Common Sense to Become a Spiritual Activist

There is a beginning to this. The contested convention has brought forth a new message of protection to be put in place that requires a better level of the Lord's presence. It is needed because of the new level of politics that has so much room for miscalculated disagreements that the prince of darkness plans to wait for in order to make a problem that can and must be stopped before it starts. That is what we are to stand against; the enemy that cannot be seen. Believe it to know the God given power you will have over it thanks to our Lord.

This is a part of a rescue mission for individuals who are already trapped in a state of mind that is awaiting an opportunity to present an exit of negativity in their actions, but only by one dimension that can be found only in the presence of a spiritual warfare state of mind that they are locked into already.

This is a gathering of different levels of people. The gathering is to prevent and protect others from harming themselves and others. This process of growth is to rescue those who have been lost out of a state of reality and do not even know it. This knowledge helps free them from this state of being.

Unfortunately, there are some Americans who look for a reason to act like humanimals tearing up and down the lifestyles that others have built. There are some people who feel they need a reason and others who feel they have enough of one because of the state of what is going on in the political arena at this time in history.

Therefore, to help with this kind of problem I have been writing books to give ways of understanding this. I am writing you to ask you to check out what I have done as a calling in and to my life and think about whether it may help the city and people just in case it could be an uprising of folk who are blinded to the ways of Satan's attack and the book _The Devil Passed Me By_, can keep the calm and stop a storm from happening to another brother in the body of Christ.

The best thing about the time is we are learning that every life had a reason because the Lord made it so. So what kind of seeds are you sowing, the ones to protect life or the other one?

I Like to Know if I am Right

Will the world ever know how many people have we left in spiritual prisons that needed help to get out that have to be torn out of that way of life in some kind of tragedy? Unfortunately, are we leaving them in there in record breaking numbers? If so, when will we stop and does the prison rating reflect on this in a way since so many people are locked up in the USA compared to the rest of the world? Well, I think so and foremost how do we get them out of the bad kind of spiritual bondage that helps to get people in trouble in the first place because of the lack of love that may be hooked into a place of controlling people by Satan in a dormant kind of way, that is waiting to be awakened on key in a way that can't be determined by a presence of a mental state that breaks down in a conflict that takes place in a spiritual warfare? Now what could be the one way out? The love they need to know of that comes from the Lord.

In Order to Never Forget

Now we don't need to forget that one of the most important things we are doing is exposing towerism to the people who have it and others to end it in America because it has caused more trouble for the world than we can imagine and can do more harm if we don't stop it.

It may be that when a tower falls it may come down at a time when it can fall into another tower and the domino affect takes place and all try to hold each other up in one way or another in a party that may be damaging and crippling the process that the right level of work done by the people who work for the people in government along with the fact they are of a kind of non-disclosed people that need a better state of transparency. To learn more about this, you can get a copy of _Fixing What is Broken in America_.

Now who wants to hear how to improve themselves? If it is you that think you can stop the insider b.s., start with the book titled _The Devil Passed Me By_. Then take the next step by getting a copy of two of your constituents, the two senators, Trent Lott and Tom Dasche, _Crisis Point_. If you want to help the country get better and make the American people more happy, try a new level of love. It can include the process of inclusion and can help stop the process of gerrmandering.

The Lord has laid out his plan; first we must come under one accord. The people of the house of God the people on the highways byways and skyways, the law enforcement agencies on all levels, police, state troopers FBI and all others including those in the political arena are all in line to receive the blessings of peace to minimize any problems that could occur, we have made available the plan that was pointed out by the Lord.

If you have been chosen to be a forerunner: for this level of work to help bless the people by the Lord. Be thankful and claim and name it.

The people on the highways and byways that need our help they depend on the leaders and humanitarians with the body of Christ to help ease their burdens.

This level of work will create justice where some may try to create injustice against themselves or others. These people may not be aware because of not having a presence of wisdom in their life that can be used to outgrow the demonology that they are used to in their present way of living.

This is hoped to be done through the collective measures that have been put forth in the material presented by Bound to Heaven Publishing/Ministries.

Zero In - A Note from the Messenger

The thing about this process of growth is, it must not come with shortchange it does come with enough to feed the multitude. The Lord has done that through my writing.

It is as the Lord prepared his work for Satan to be known about and to people to be able to turn away from him. The Lord had to have an endless supply of food love and good news with an understanding of his gospel.

That is the reason I have written so much to teach a man how to fish. Within the will of the Lord if mankind can learn to get what the Lord has put in them out the people and the world will be better off. Will you help I thank you for all you can do to promote this body of work, Brother Bush, a man who doesn't want to see a nation of people go into mourning as others have done who experience spiritual warfare.

As a humble man, how would you handle the reality of being called to step out on blind faith, in order to level the playing field but also to put the play book together with the only ingredient that can complete it. Now what is that? That is love.

MY biggest presence of thought is to be obedient to my Lord. But it is my thought on one single process that I continue to learn, that is to love my enemy. Now I finally know what it is about; you can't help the friends of mankind in a lot of ways or in as many as you may need to unless you know how to get the enemy out of the pits of darkness also.

More About the Author

Can I be one of the priests of the night who God has taught to fight for mankind on a level of not seeing or hearing but feeling in the heart of mankind to love?

It is time to start to snatch back more souls than ever that are in line to be haunted or executed by Satan.

The awesome work that all involved will have to do is believe and promote the books and if you see anyone out of line with this state of peacefulness, talk to them. If they won't retreat or stop the process of upsetting the status quo in the wrong way, call the right authorities if they are not around. Then you make sure you are taking the right steps before you make a citizen's arrest. That should be the last action you take life or harm is about to come to someone you may not have another choice to add to the process of stopping someone.

I have worked in the field of protecting people at hospitals, schools and other facilities. I feel that the training I have in the spiritual field of training gives me more to make use of in ways that can help me then some others because of mother and father wit alongside common sense with the Lord's intuition that has sustained me this far as a man.

There are four groups of people
that make a whole unit to share with

Ministers and clergy to recruit from churches alongside the entire body of Christ, to help eliminate the satanic forces that have been put in place;

Law enforcement - to make up a unified team of individuals to be on one accord to deliver a blow of justice against any force trying to create chaos or confusion at the upcoming convention;

Politicians; and

Public at large, including media outlets.

All of these make up a whole to not only give exposure but to recruit individuals from all walks of life to participate in the upcoming event to stop harm from taking place in our society.

Learn it to Give it

It is time to become the one that is rest-filled in order to not become one who is in the restless sea of darkness that is mad because it has no light. The blindness that has to remain is not of your doing. It is you have light. Therefore, let it not become a permanent place that keeps you there.

That is why knowing the way to go with wisdom that can sustain the ability so all can live.

Now is this what Satan puts in a person the lack of love and not knowing they have it. Also because the Lord has an endless supply he always gives out. But when people forget or don't know it that may or will knock them off balance but at the same time, they don't know. Does it help us to show it to someone that is in darkness? I do and you may need to also.

What a way to learn the facts that, at the end of one journey there begins another. Knowing the way to go with wisdom can sustain the ability so all can live. The real journey begins at the end of the books that are prepared for you to read.

A part of the writing in this presentation of information came out of the _All Peoples Handbook_ to help inspire you to know it is not of a man's will that it has been written but of a heavenly pathway it has to give people a way to see if they can discover if they have spiritual skills.

The Eye Drops are to Open the Eyes

We must treat this journey as if the cobra is dead. Because the bird that makes contact on an eye to eye level with a cobra paralyzes the bird and the bird looks at its death but doesn't move. Now, if we consider the death of someone else as if they are the bird at first and Satan is the snake, is the cobra, that is dead on a level of we can't see into its darkness any way we find freedom for those who are trapped in the darkness.

What may be considered as the greatest fear of all is the fear of no love that does more harm in life than anything I believe this is where Satan is at in its existence of the time and wants company because it is jealous of all humans as he was in heaven. So how many can see the cobra dead so others can see their life they have to live?

We as a people can get more than one thing done with this vision of the life we have that inspires love.

Now one other thing, it is said that no weapons formed against us shall prosper, but it did not say no weapons will be formed against us or won't exist. Therefore, be aware and vigilant.

The ways we can start to head off a possible future crisis shouldn't be limited to the star war practice of thinking. We can and should be able to use the blue print of our DNA on a level of spiritual guidance, to help us to deal with the upcoming event with a level of protection.

Have I been given the blessing regarding the upcoming convention or am I just using common sense?

Can we all Just Keep in Mind
That the Great Power is Coming?

We at Bound to Heaven Publishing/Ministries are a part of the al souls matter and we know that it is the gateway to the spirit-man, it is to believe that all people have the best treasures and jewels down inside of their living being that is protected by their eternal being. Our goal is to get people to love their life and regurgitate it to share with the people of the world to make it better.

That is the way to go to know that all life matters. Do the dance with peace in your heart on a peaceful wellness in the eyes of righteousness for eternity.

Just imagine if you get this much of a new presence of thought out of what is a forerunner that is only the invitation to what a full ticket has to bring forth that can supply you in enough ways to brighten the days ahead of you and at the same time you will have a cup that is running over.

The fact is, this present state of knowledge that has come into focus has a lot to offer but there is one thing to rest assure about it is not of a religious based group, it is the development of spiritual growth process of love from its beginning to its end; enlightenment.

Ending this Part of Hell that has
Affected Mankind Much too Long

We can put the fire out to stop the brimstones from smoldering and quench the embers out to not be able to jump to another place or level to start another kind of fire. To stop the negativity from landing on the earth that is been hanging up in a high place and land on people when they least expect it.

Stopping the clashing of the spirit so there are many people who think they have the right connection with their spirit man but they don't. So don't get in because you think you fit in; you may not belong. Know your place by way of the Lord's placement procedures.

We as a people are our best defense against the foolish, who want to try to harm us and this is a way to break into a supernatural state of creating oversight, to protect the people and the land.

Is this a Warning or Premonition of Something to Come?

Has the love I have for over 40 years of writing been put with the right connection, so you get the right protection: by the Lord?

Is This an Illusion or Reality?

There are all kinds of new perspectives on the state of governing the country. Can we truly see a better pathway that will make us able to not go back down the same ones we have been down before? I am referring to the ghosts of Chicago and the past violence that reared up so mightily in 1968.

If we look at this in the presence of a parallel universal, when Donald Trump visited the city and it seemed to have become electrified in a sense to regurgitate a haunting spirit of violence to a certain measure where even he had to cancel his rally. At the same time, could spirits of darkness be embellishing around him out of sight until they can rear up again and influence others that are not aware they are there? This could happen by them coming to Cleveland to help insight the spiritual warfare that can land up on the people in the presence of the RNC. Just a thought that may help you keep it real in your own way of thinking.

Now is a Great Time

Now is a great time to prevent the beginning of a mountain's growth that can be turned into a molehill. This is the process of taking the wind out of the sails of a ship that is propelled by the ill winds of ungodliness. If you care anything about the city, the people and the land we live in, join in to help. There is a calling to make this one of the greatest performances that mankind has ever presented to the people in the body of Christ to be witnessed by the heavenly body of the Lord. Therefore, if you are too proud to stand for this, get on your knees and pray for it.

What could be the worst part of some people who are dishonorable to themselves? They are so afraid of coming out of their self-contained environment, it hurts them like no other person can hurt or harm them. How sad is it for a person to lock themselves out of their own life from living within the shadow of them and a life they could have?

It took me to stumble on a kind of bonanza to realize that in the past I got by a fear to live once I knew that Satan wanted me to hurt myself and it was not me who I thought it was. That made me angry and I know the only way to pay Satan for the fear I had keep living, saying amen.

Do you want to help untie
the city from an ungodly fate?

Again I will say, A call is going out to all ministry leaders, members of the clergy and people in the body of Christ. There may be a charge on our hearts to complete a challenge of the development of the will of the Lord in our spirit to show our love for him as our brothers' keepers.

There is not much time left to get as many soldiers of Christ involved in the upcoming battle. We must be prepared to know how to win this battle. That is right, it is a fight and we must know that the victory is already won through Christ Jesus.

Now what does this challenge require? It is to not fight the fight. It is to keep the people out of it and not fuel it or bring forth any kind of wick to set off powder kegs. It is a war of peace and love to help people come down from the highway and skyway of their warring states of spirit, to keep them from inciting a spiritual war, that Satan wants to take place so he can get in it to win it because mankind becomes lost and confused and has no idea what he is doing and how he got there and how they have no chance to win something started by Satan. They haven't got the sense to get out of the way in time in order for the Lord to do what he does to clear the air.

This is what was done in heaven at the time of the rebellion of the first spiritual war ever. To the new wise men, and the kings and queens, it is time to stop this abuse on the people in the lands. May the calling to become watchmen see its way out of your heart.

To know or not know

How prevalent is the work we are
doing in the body of Christ?

If anyone does not know the Lord's way of his working in an orderly fashion when it is right before their spiritual sight, then they may need to go back to the drawing board and ask the Lord's forgiveness, along with teaching them to not forget to be humble to the people he may use in their presence, like it or not!

It is time to get the people off of the edge with a message from the word. Please don't let the people hook themselves to this wagon. It is a bondage that mankind can stand free from the fight or battle whether they are one in it, or a multitude, in one of the most vicious warring factors that mankind faces daily and loses. It can be a matter of life and death for a multitude of people, not just one.

How many believe that we are facing a state of crisis? If you are one, then let it be known if you believe in the power of the Lord, the crisis resulting from the fear some people have, will pass us by and the daytime nightmares that some people have subjected themselves to, through their limited way of thinking, can and will disappear in the name of Jesus, Amen.

Do we as people know what we are really being invited to and have invited to the city we live in? Yes, people with money to spend is good but the devil in disguise is coming also, and we do not want to talk about it or believe to a degree that it exists. Oh well, it does and Satan is looking for a fight. Believe it or not, he wants to recruit as many people as he can and he wants you to win for his side. That is what Satan does every time you hear of an ungodly death. Now, do you have the will to stand up to him and say it is no longer about you? The people have suffered long enough and the dead cries out from the grave. Do not stay blind any longer!

Now to get back to his latest fight, it is the spiritual war he wants to start within the RNC, one of the biggest events he has plans for, which he wants to include you in. We as people can win it with the Lord on our side. We can take down Satan if we do what God said. Instructions are as follows.

The book titled *The Devil Passed Me By*, gives you the complete blueprint of how this is done. Warning, without the instructions, if we as a people go into a fight about whatever decision we think is right or wrong about this event it will not matter, because we are setting ourselves up for a big loss.

There is a plan of action that requires the wisdom of the people to use. Without it you may be lost in a dimension of destruction that you will bring upon yourself and others. I would like for you to think about this before you do anything.

If Satan fought angels in heaven and got through it, even though he was kicked out, how in the hell do you think you can fight with him and win, when he has so many years of experience? How foolish can we be as humans? I hope not that foolish.

To bring it out of the street some people need to learn to not let Satan kick their ass all the way to and through hell. When you fight against your fellow man, it may not be you doing the fighting it can be Satan using you like you are his bitch to do something for him. Now, who is the man or woman and are you someone's bitch who is getting pimped by the lowest creature that lives in spirit? It is on the planet and hasn't changed but gotten worse. It can't be seen but still is a snake. It is in the invisible spiritual realm where it bites and poisons people.

Do you as a person know how to bear arms and what armor to use when it only requires love? There is one more thing to say to Satan. We in the body of Christ demand that he let our people go because he shall not win this war!

Help to end the fear some people have that is a part of winning God's warfare to be a part of sharing in the glory of the victory.

This is one of the greatest ways to grow up as a child of God to be able to eat meat and vegetables that are prepared for you daily. Utilize the tools that you can when Satan tries to bring you down. I have learned that my anger toward the way he has tried to use me in the past by presenting the different fear factors that he has at one time instilled upon the atmosphere in my life were harmful.

Once I realized this, I turned this around and became harmful to its presence in my life with the wisdom the Lord has provided.

We can dismantle and disassemble Satan's war machine that he has put in our presence with the tools the Lord has given us.

Now to help anyone who feels they cannot handle this process of growth, just ask the Lord to handle it for you, it is as simple as that!

As a Forget-Me-Not

This presence of theology can be used as a safeguard where there may be a multitude of people gathered with disagreements that are subject to get out of control. That can stop and/or head off a spiritual warfare by befriending them with its earthly presence.

What are some people's, who find themselves in a difficult situation, biggest problem? They don't know how to fight fair to win and are so much of a sore loser it is crazy what they try to (or may try to) create afterward. What can be done about this? Pray and find the right books that can teach you how to fight fair and lose when you have to, without being sore. It is better to stay your own friend when you do the right thing and believe it or not there are some people that would rather not be their own friend if it means losing a fight.

How many people are walking around that have become strangers to them self because of this fact alone? I say stop it because it isn't that serious to keep yourself on the outside of yourself, looking at times at someone you can't trust or think of as a real friend.

What can you do? Pray for help and search it out. It's not like you are praying for rain.

This certifies that (insert your name here) has committed to the dedication of the government and will take on the posture as a non-violent person at all times during the political debates. I will show the American people the best level of caring for my fellow man that I find myself in the presence of, whether I like their point of view or not.

The time has come to stop all stages of backbiting. This is not a horse race and we can act like we are civilized because we represent the people and if we can't do this right we should like for another job and that's a fact!

People need to stop acting like they are being treated so unfairly. It is a mythological excuse that people come up with to do the wrong thing, whether it is done to help someone or not. It is a part of drama that plays out during a time when someone says, "I need your help and if I don't get it you are responsible for my bleeding heart."

People need to get for real because one day on earth or not you get your real pay forever since you play in life. It gets examined and the profiling you have done gets stripped of all makeup and your true appearance is shown to the best audience in the entire universe. Therefore, if you are faking the funk and not being for real, pack your bags and quit your job. It is better to quit something you are not good at now than before you are dead. Let's be honest, there is nothing like a second chance. Therefore, you can now live in peace.

Here is an opening to a new beginning for your life to share your love, don't steal, kill, sell, trade or buy it. Cherish it and it will cherish you also.

Too many ethics choke the view out of the point or could it be the person is too full of sh___. Don't be one who is full of it!

Thank you for sticking around for the new changing of the guard. It is a planned process to know that the old, stale way of the congressional system can give the American people a new kind of outlook in a way that doesn't repeat itself or reflect the outlook that others may not like. It may leave them something to look forward to in their future by the way they see us conduct ourselves in a newly acceptable country.

When all is said and done, they see we will get the job done that they (and we) at times didn't know whether we could or not, it seems. In retrospect it is the pursuit of happiness that we as Americans really want. Therefore, we lift our spirit to the sky and in our hearts we sing out, "Oh thank the Lord He loves America and its people from sea to shining sea."

In Life We can Change

No one ever needs to try to be the best crook because they have a law that will let them by to buy a better way out of trouble as they play the game of politricks.

In Retrospect

It seems as if there is nothing so far from the truth than the fact that being a servant of the people has turned into a vendetta between politicians to see if one can create a level of success that outmatches the other. If we look at it in layman terminology, it seems as if it is a process that has put the people in a dimension where they are stuck without seeing much progress.

Let us not keep ourselves stuck in an imponderable/ponderable place. Is this a word that can go across the end of time and still stay still. In other words, do not become homogenized. It is time to redefine the exploration of involving a rapidly changing world in the logistics and eliminate all of the ethics that make no sense at all.

This will become a part of signs that are to be placed to see around town, with logos on them saying "Bound to Heaven Publishing/Ministries loves you" and "thank you for not being a part of the party pooper's plans."

We are recruiting persuaders to spoil the plans Satan has to be a party pooper that poops all over people.

We are ready the devil may try to rise up against the people who stand for the body of Christ but they will fail.

We Have so Many Wonderful Things
Going on Here That are Good

We can have free Hurst rides available if you like. If you aren't the one for peace and intend to make trouble, it might help change your mind.

People don't be a sag get God business right before you put on your swagger.

Welcome to a Development of a More Cultured Understanding Between two Generations: Old and New!

M-N
Know the Cheap Way
If you cheapen your life, it will show in your life skills.

Let the Lord

Catch you before you try to; It is better for all.

Watch the Atmosphere

It does change on your behalf no buts about it.

Americans

We do all this in agreement with the will of the Lord in order to let out faith be showed as we would in a baptism to let the people and world know we believe that the Lord has always bless America and will keep doing so.

The priceless principals that can become like the Northern Star, that led the way out of slavery for a people has reopened in a way that is color blind. It will give guidance to a part of the free world. Once it gets started, it can become infectious so it will spread through the whole world to help bless humanity.

Why do some people act like they don't have a lick of sense in them? I think it is because Satan has them fool themselves that everything they do can be made right, whatever it is!

This may seem like a little book, but it will have the effects of a freedom bell that can be heard around the world. It will forever ring once the people, who can best magnify it, have it in hand, in order for it to ring out glory, glory, glory hallelujah!

As a presentation I would like everyone to use this as a follow up exam to show how you will grade yourself with the work that only the Lord can pay you for, in his way. Therefore, the grade you wind up with can only be given by you with your ability to see the rest of this plan of action through to the end.

The Lord doesn't require a grand amount of people to get what he wants done but he may want you.

The work we do in the body of Christ will not be in vain. One of the hottest tickets in town is in this book!

Psalms 119:74 – Those who fear Y will be glad when they see me, because I have hoped in Your word.

Psalms 27:11 – Teach me Your way, O Lord, and lead me in a smooth path, because of my enemies.

Psalms 37:7-9 – Rest in the Lord, and wait patiently for Him; do not fret because of him who prospers in his way, because of the man who brings wicked schemes to pass. Cease from anger, and forsake wrath; do not fret – it only causes harm. For evildoers shall be cut off; but those who wait on the Lord, they shall inherit the earth.

Psalms 62:5 – My soul, wait silently for God alone, for my expectation is from Him.

Isaiah 64:4 – For since the beginning of the world men have not heard nor perceived by the ear, nor has the eye seen any God besides You, who acts for the one who waits for Him.

Your Notes

_____

_____

_____

_____

_____

_____

_____

_____

_____

_____

_____

_____

_____

_____

Philippians 4:17 – not that I seek the gift, but I seek the fruit that abounds to your account.

Acts 20:24 – But none of these things move me; nor do I count my life dear to myself, so that I may finish my race with joy, and the ministry which I received from the Lord Jesus, to testify to the gospel of the grace of God.

www.ingramcontent.com/pod-product-compliance
Lightning Source LLC
Chambersburg PA
CBHW061951280526
45787CB00004B/1815